the book book

Bringing Book Arts to Scrapbooking

Carol Wingert

Debbie Crouse

Janelle Smith

Tena Sprenger

Renee Camacho

Sarah Fishburn

Ruth Giauque

contents

welcome

In *The Book Book*, you'll find a collection of the freshest ideas in circulation—ideas that marry the world of book arts with the world of scrapbooking. Our talented group of artists have bridged the gap by combining their passion for photos and memories with the adventure of creating their own books. Our goal is to inspire you and share the adventure.

Inside these pages you will find books incorporated into clever scrapbook layouts. Layouts that will change the way you think about scrapbooking forever.

You'll also find that creating mini layouts in books of your own making is a totally liberating experience. Gone are the "rules" of scrapbooking in the larger format of a traditionally bound album. You make the binding, so you make the rules. Join us as we begin the adventure...

1 Books, Incorporated

Study the Dewey Decimal System—the system used to classify and arrange books—and nowhere will you find a number that places books on a scrapbook page. But our artists have broken the rules and created books of all types to incorporate onto layouts to house additional photos, journaling and memorabilia. Peruse these pages and master how to take books from the shelf to your scrapbook pages. With such clever ideas, maybe Mr. Dewey will add another decimal to his system!

Jagger BY JANELLE

the process

For the "Favorites" book, machine stitch down two sides of a piece of cardstock. Make a mini book from cardstock and hold the pages together with an eyelet. Slide in place behind the sewn cardstock. For the "Nicknames" book, bind strips of cardstock with waxed linen and slip inside a corrugated cardboard pocket that has been hand stitched to the layout. For the "Firsts" mini book, cut a strip of cardstock to fit inside the box, then fold accordion style. Adhere the front and back flaps of the mini book to the lid and base of the box. For the "Milestones" book, cut tags to fit the pocket on the page. Bind together by first wrapping wire around a pencil to make a spiral. Punch holes at the top of the book, then thread the wire spiral through the holes.

VARIATIONS: Use mini books inserted in pockets, boxes, etc. to record memories about a child's first year. Mini books are an excellent way to give more detailed descriptions about who or what the page is about. They also bring an interactive element and add dimension to a layout.

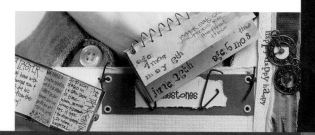

Our Vancouver Mess

BY RENEE

THE PROCESS

Create a miniature photo accordion by punching several photos into squares and sewing them together to create a folded accordion. Adhere each book to a square collage and close with ribbon.

IDEA TO NOTE: Renee created a file folder that flips open to showcase photos and journaling.

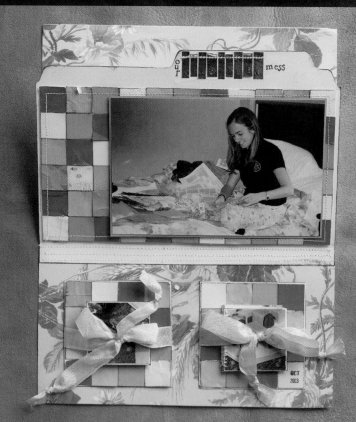

Discovering Age Two BY CAROL

THE PROCESS

STEP 1: Adhere the bottom front of one envelope to the open back flap of another. Continue to add envelopes, adhering the flap to the envelope front until desired size is reached. **STEP 2:** When dry, accordion-fold envelopes so the envelope with the unglued flap is on top. Secure with ribbon, twill or twine. **STEP 3:** Fill envelopes with photos, letters, quotations or other memorabilia.

VARIATIONS: This project makes a great travel journal to house tickets, pamphlets, etc. For an alternate project, add a book board cover to the front flap and another piece to the back of the last envelope. Cover with decorative papers. Finish the book board edges with a silver or gold leafing pen. Use ribbon, twill or twine to tie the book together. The end result? An accordion-folded envelope book!

5

Faces by You BY RENEE

the process

Decorate each page of a small archival photo album insert with walnut ink, rubber stamps and photos. Attach the book to the layout with adhesive and snaps. Finish off each page with turn tabs.

Destination Florida BY TENA

THE PROCESS

Fold two pieces of 8 1/2" x 11" paper in half lengthwise to make the cover and pages. Use a bone folder to make sure the pages fold easily. Score all pages 1/2" from the spine. Use an awl to pierce holes 1/2" from spine. Sew the pages together with a tapestry needle and fiber. Mount photos on pages using oversized slide mounts that have been inked with brown ink and embossed with clear embossing powder. Create closure using fibers and a button.

VARIATIONS: This is a great way to scrapbook more photos than would normally fit on one layout to celebrate a birthday, holiday or family gathering. This structure could also be used as a storybook that includes photos about the subject.

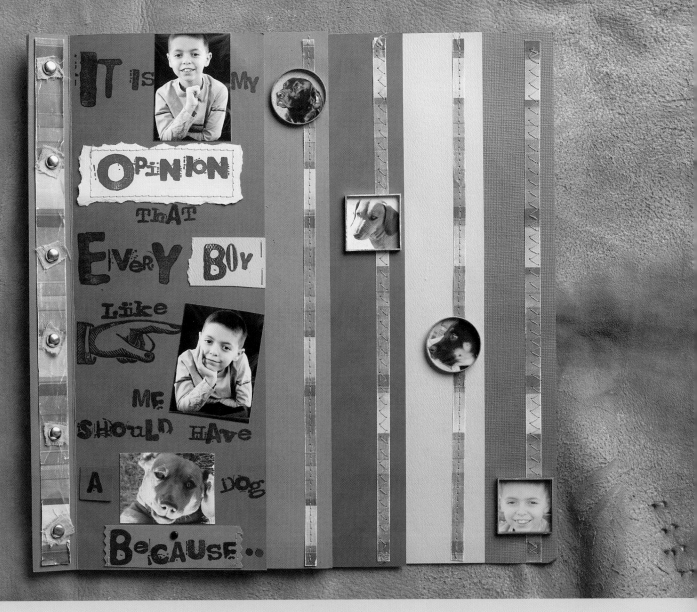

IT IS MY OPINION THAT EVERY BOY LIKE ME SHOULD HAVE A DOG BECAUSE...

Every Boy Should Have a Dog BY TENA

To create a graduated photo album right on your layout, take five pieces of cardstock with the largest piece being 12" x 12". Range widths 2" a part on the other four pieces from 5" to 10". Stack the cardstock, putting the largest piece on the back. Score all pages 1/2" from edge. Punch six holes down the left side of all the pages. Hold pages together with brads. For added texture, add a frayed square of muslin under each brad.

VARIATIONS: This type of scrapbook page could also be used to tell a story using the stepped pages to denote separate chapters in the book. So instead of framed photos on the page edges, include chapter titles and numbers.

IF I HAD MY OWN DOG

I would never be lonely

MY DOG WOULD BE WITH ME

HUG

HOLD

SNUGGLE

A Boys Best Friend is his Dog

SO Please

Pretty Please with sugar

PLEASE

Please!

Can I have my own dog?

Third Grade

BY TENA

THE PROCESS

Paint a crayon box white. When dry, sponge on ink, then ink the edges black. Stamp title on the front, then seal with matte Mod Podge. Measure cardstock cards to fit inside and set an eyelet in one corner. Embellish, then string bead chain through the eyelets. Store in box.

VARIATIONS: This box could also be altered to house baseball cards on a sports-themed page or used to hold mini postcards, travel photos and ephemera on a travel-themed page.

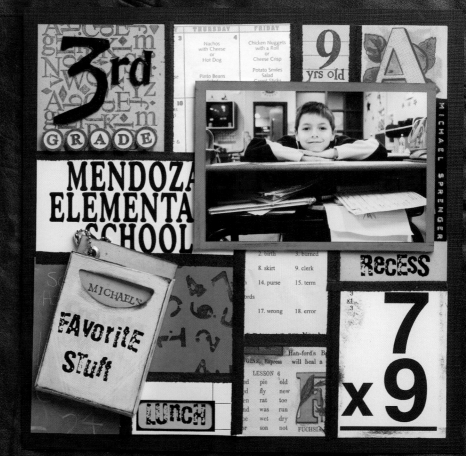

Little Bump

BY JANELLE

the process

To create the mini book, adorn cardboard covers with a printed transparency. Use metal hinges to hold the book together. Attach to the page using printed twill, ribbon or a chain.

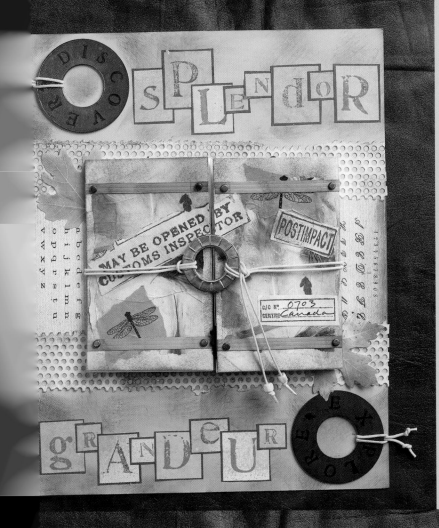

Splendor and Grandeur

BY CAROL

the process

Purchase or make two accordion fold books to fit on a layout. Create page background, then lay books side-by-side so a gatefold book is created. Adhere ribbon, twill or twine to the back of the accordions before attaching to layout.

VARIATIONS: To make a "stand alone" gatefold accordion book, cut a piece of cardstock (or book board for a heavier back) the same size as two side-by-side accordions. Ribbon, twill or twine should be inserted between the solid back piece and the two accordion pieces. Glue layers together and proceed with completing covers and interiors.

Brand New Me

the process

BY TENA

To create the large matchbook, cut cardstock to 4 1/2" x 6 1/2". Cut another piece to 4 1/2" x 9" for the back. Taper one end of the longer piece and fold over to create a flap. Cut two slits on the front cover to slide flap for closure. Insert pages and bind with a prong fastener.

VARIATIONS: Use this matchbook as a stand-alone mini book or gift book.

Hollywood Romance

BY RUTH

THE PROCESS

To create a gatefold book, punch 1/8" holes down one side of the postcards. (Punch half of the postcards on the left and half on the right.) Cut a piece of cardstock to the same height as the cards and 3/8" wider. Hole punch the cardstock on the left and right sides. Attach the postcards to their respective sides with beaded jump rings.

VARIATIONS: This book would make a clever mini travel album by using postcards from a vacation.

the process Hana BY RUTH ▾

Create a meandering tag book by attaching several tags together with ribbon so they will fold together to make a stack. When opened, the tags should fold out one and two at a time to reveal the inside pages.

VARIATION: Try replacing the tags with photos or greeting cards.

Baby Delanie BY CAROL ▴

Hinge four cardstock pieces of varying sizes to the sides of an 8" square of cardstock, so when folded in, they fit within the square. Embellish with papers, photos, paint and stamps.

Hailing from Asia, accordion books were invented as an alternative to unwieldy papyrus and parchment scrolls. Our inventive artists have turned this ancient concept into a more modern edition. Today, accordion fold books provide a quick and easy alternative to a large, unwieldy scrapbook album. Each fold creates a blank page awaiting your photos and creativity; and because the pages are smaller, completing an album takes no time at all, no matter how you fold it!

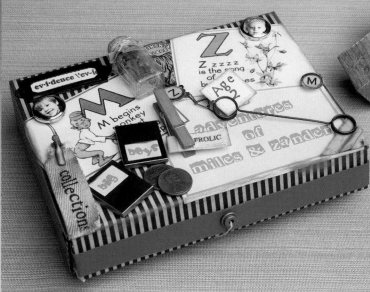

The Adventures of Zander & Miles
BY JANELLE
THE PROCESS

Accordion fold paper, then trace a photo cut out on the top fold. Being careful not to cut through the fold, cut out to create a paper-doll accordion book. Affix inside an embellished box.

VARIATIONS: Instead of using one photo, cut several photos and bind them into an accordion book. This book could showcase a family (one photo of each member) or an action sequence using photos of the same person doing a series of actions (dancing, jumping, etc.).

Exploring Las Vegas BY RENEE

the process

Cover a ready-made accordion book with patterned papers. Use a matte finish paper adhesive to seal the cover and protect it from handling. To create the closure, punch two holes on opposite sides of the back cover. String elastic with binding edges through the holes and loop around a button that has been sewn or wired onto the top cover.

VARIATIONS: Other ideas for closing accordion books include the following: tie a ribbon around the entire book for a quick and easy closure; attach that same ribbon through a hole in the back cover for a more secure closure, having it come together on top to tie; create latches for both sides of the album; create button/loop closure on both sides; or attach ribbons on each side of the album, closing the sides.

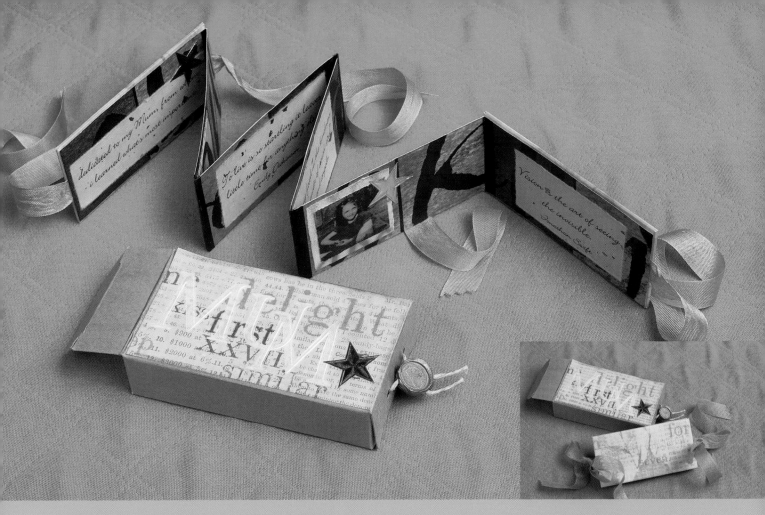

For My Mum BY SARAH

For the covers, cut cardboard into two 2" x 4" pieces, then cover with patterned paper and vellum. Create an accordion fold panel to put between the covers. Sarah cut paper so there were five panels totaling approximately 20" for the front and three sections totaling approximately 12" for the back. Adhere the two pieces together, affixing the extra panel on each end to the covers. Place a length of ribbon between each cover and end paper to make the closure. Add a strip of black graphic arts tape to each fold. Embellish the pages with quotations and photos. Slip inside an altered box.

VARIATIONS: Write a story about a day in the life of your children and include photos or have them draw pictures. A larger version of this book would be a fabulous way to showcase recipes or bits of advice to a new bride or mother.

Freedom
BY CAROL

Paint playing cards with white gesso. Allow to dry, then paint over them with brown, allowing some of the white to show through. Cover cards with photos, journaling and related elements. Set eyelets on opposite ends of all cards, except the first and last, which will have eyelets on only one side. Tie cards together with waxed linen and fold accordion style. Insert cards into an embellished tin.

VARIATIONS: This type of book is a great way to use loose game cards at the bottom of the toy box. Create mini stories on the small-scale panel, insert into small coin envelopes or add to scrapbook layouts.

Waiting for the Train
BY CAROL

the process

Cut three 4 1/2" x 6 1/2" panels from cardstock or use a pre-folded three-panel accordion book. Cut oval, circle or square shapes into two of the panels. Make the first shape larger than the one on panel #2 to create a tunnel-like appearance. Glue a photo to the last page. Add fragments of photos and various elements to the cut out panels. Attach the panels accordion style with hinges, ties or strips of tape. Create a three part gatefold folio out of book board. Cover each section individually, then bind together with electrical tape. Glue tunnel book to the inside back section of the folio. Line up the bottom of the accordions with the bottom of the folio so the book can stand up straight. Create a tie out of a railroad crossing sign and twill.

School Days BY CAROL
THE PROCESS

Create or purchase two 3" x 5" accordion books (six panels per book). Decorate the pages. Stitch the accordions together – back-to-back – with a pamphlet stitch in the valley folds only. The mountain folds will pop out on each side of the book. Cut two pieces of book board to 6" x 5" and cover with decorative paper or fabric. Glue the front cover to the first two blank ends of the accordions and the back cover to the last two ends.

To do a pamphlet stitch, use an awl to pierce three equally spaced holes in the valley folds. Thread unwaxed linen thread through the center hole (either side of the book). Leave a 3-4" tail with no knot at this time. Thread through the top hole, then thread through bottom hole and bring up through the center hole again. Position the tail threads so one is on one side of the long thread and the other tail is on the opposite side. Tie tails together in a square knot, cut off long ends and dab knot with a tiny bit of glue.

VARIATIONS: This book is a great way to show a progression of events or, as in this case, the growth of a child. It is also a great way to show contrast (i.e. the difference between a boy and a girl, or "He Said, She Said" book).

My Family Connections

BY CAROL

To make an accordion book, either measure and fold panels or repeatedly fold a long panel in half. Burnish the folds with a bone folder for crisp, even folds. Decorate the inside pages with various clothing and jewelry connectors to create a "connections" theme. Remember when sewing a zipper into an accordion book, the space taken by the zipper will need to be cut out of the panel. Cover two book boards with kraft paper, then embellish. Use for the front and back cover.

THE PRO

3 The Extremes

According to Guinness World Records, the smallest book ever printed measures a mere .9 x .9 mm. With 11 lines of text per page, it's a wonder how Russian author Anton Chekhov made it all fit! While the books in this chapter won't require a microscope, the artists explore extremes in bookmaking with big and small, large and tiny—the mini and the maxi. They prove that nothing is too big or too small for this craft. So be an extremist, dream big (and small!) and try something you never thought possible by creating your own sizeable book of art.

Faces of My Family
BY CAROL

Punch photos with a circle punch and adhere to metal-rimmed tags. Position tags into a plus sign shape. Adhere ribbon to the backs of the tags, so all the tags are interconnected in a grid pattern. Allow about 1/4" to 3/8" of space between tags to allow for movement. Cover the back of each tag with paper. To fold, bring tags on the edges into the center line of tags. Alternate folding back and forth from top to bottom until tags are in one stack. Place in decorated tin.

VARIATIONS: This book makes a fabulous Mom or Grandma brag book since it's small and sturdy. It would also make a great paperweight for a desk or an accessory for a coffee table.

THE PROCESS

Little Miss Millie BY JANELLE

Lay out dominos in the desired order, then adhere ribbon to the back of each so the "book" will open accordion style. Age the dominos with chalk ink. Add photos and words printed on transparencies. A great way to use your tiny index prints from your photo processor.

little miss millie sat on her horsey eating her pbrj

along came a spider who crawled

down beside her and frightened miss millie away.

France
Travel Journal

BY CAROL

the process

Cut chipboard pages to fit inside the lid. Fill pages with travel photos, ephemera, etc. Punch oval-shaped holes near the top and bottom of each page. Thread ribbon through the holes to connect the pages. Glue a piece of ribbon to the back of the last panel. The ribbon should be long enough to bring around to the front and tie. Adhere last page to the lid. Fold pages accordion style. Secure with the ribbon. On the other side of the box, create an assemblage of travel memorabilia. Finish the edges of the box with ribbon and upholstery tacks. Idea to note: Carol incorporated other book styles on several of the pages. The Eiffel Tower page includes a mini book under the metal plate.

Cut davey board into two 13" squares and one 1/4" x 13" strip. Lay handmade paper face down and place the three davey board pieces in the middle with about 1/8" space between each. Mark where the boards should be placed. Remove pieces, then cover one piece with PVA. Place on paper where marked. Repeat with the two other pieces. Turn the entire piece over and smooth with a brayer. Trim paper around the outside of the boards, leaving a 1/2" border. Fold edges in and adhere with PVA. Cut a piece of paper to fit the entire interior spread.

the process

Spread PVA across the entire interior surface, being sure to apply adhesive in the spaces between each davey board piece. Lay paper in place and smooth with a brayer. Reinforce the adhesion in the spaces by pressing with the edge of a ruler. Embellish cover. Add album pages complete with 10" x 10" enlargements.

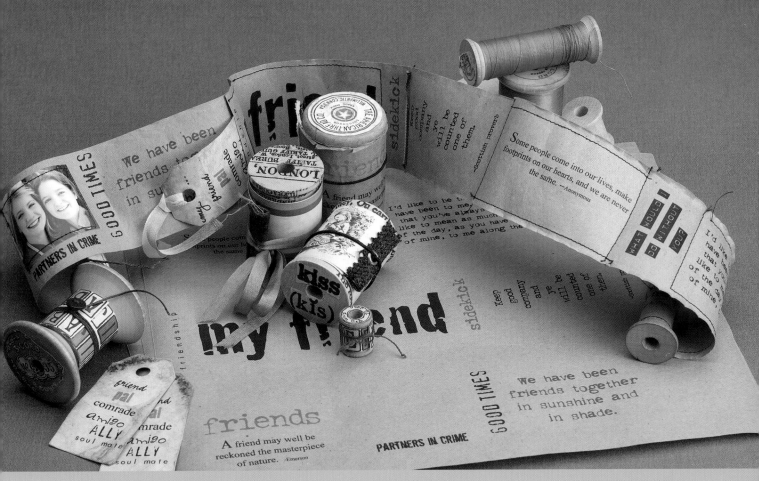

Spool Book BY DEBBIE

Decoupage spools with tissue paper or leave original labels. Arrange words in a document, so when cut apart, they can be spliced together to form a scroll. Print on brown kraft paper. Cut into widths to fit spools, stitch ends together and embellish with flat ephemera. Glue one end to the spool and sew a piece of fabric to the other end. Close with an eyelet and barbed elastic or ribbon, or with a button and waxed linen.

Tooth Fairy BY TENA

THE PROCESS

Paint the inside and outside of an oversized matchbox. Stamp top of matchbox with alphabet stamps and glue envelope and watchmaker tin to the bottom. Insert drawer pulls into both ends.

For the mini book, cut small tags from cardstock and clip together with a brad. Make pop-ups between pages to show photos, and rubber stamp poem on the pages. Attach door knockers to the front and back, thread ribbon through each one and tie closed. Store in the matchbox.

VARIATIONS: This project would be a cute way to give a special piece of jewelry, keys to a new car or money. The mini book could tell the story or share the sentiment. It would also be a charming to take a smaller matchbox and insert jump rings in the top of the box so a child could wear it as a necklace.

4 Unexpected Elements

Prehistoric man scrawled on the walls of his cave. The Greeks and Romans made a leap forward in book technology by hinging wooden tablets in a book-like fashion. Our artists are making a leap of their own by tossing out the rules and creating books with anything they can lay their hands on. From license plates to lunch bags, it's all fair game when it comes to making books in the 21st century.

Band-Aid for the Hurt
BY CAROL

Sand a vintage tin. Paint with white gesso and stipple with brown gesso to age. Leave the word "Band-Aid" partially exposed. Paint charms with white and brown gesso to age. Secure title block with surgical tape. Create a mini accordion book to fit inside the tin. Secure the pages together with round adhesive bandages.

VARIATIONS: Make a brightly colored get-well book for someone with a long term illness. Use chocolate or candy tins for a "sweetness" theme or use a holiday tin to hold a book recapping the holidays.

Radman's Tag Book
BY JANELLE

Line up the holes of one large tag and six small tags, making sure the bottom of the large tag and bottom of the small tags are facing opposite directions. Fold the large tag around the small tags. Punch a hole through the back of the large tag behind the existing holes, then thread a ribbon through all holes to secure. Tuck the bottom of the large tag under the top to make a matchbook-style book.

Grandma's Brag Book
BY JANELLE

Create a large tag from cardstock, then fold into three sections. (The sections do not have to be equal.) Create a mini book for the inside from folded strips of cardstock. Sew the book into the tag by poking two holes through the center seam of the book pages and through the spine of the cover. Thread waxed linen through the holes, tying a knot on the exterior of the tag. Add photos, mementos and journaling to pages. For a closure, thread an elastic through the hole, then loop it around a hook that has been sewn to the cover.

Family Road Trip
BY TENA

Use a band saw or tin snips to cut a standard sized license plate into three pieces (front and back cover and spine piece). Cut piano hinges to the appropriate length. Round sharp edges of the license plate using a metal file. Use a rivet gun, washers and 3/16" rivets to attach piano hinges to cover and spine. Assemble the book. Rivet a 6" ring-closure mechanism into the spine. Drill additional holes into the spine and cover for charms and embellishments. Rivet a closure onto front and back cover. Cover the inside of the plate with map paper. Create interior pages from paper and embellish with travel ephemera and photos.

VARIATIONS: Use this format to create a memory book of an antique car (using an antique license plate) or to remember a first car or someone's car collection. Consider leaving two license plates in tact, drilling holes on the left side, binding with book rings and filling with panoramic pages and photos.

the
process

Go Fight Win
BY TENA

Disassemble a pre-made locker book, keeping only the front and back covers. Decorate locker with stickers and memorabilia and insert photos and journaling. To better support the heavy elements, adhere a piece of chipboard to the back of the layout.

VARIATIONS: Cruise through an office supply or book store, looking for small, unique binders that can be taken apart and rebuilt on scrapbook pages. Mini composition books are another small notebook that can be altered and attached to a scrapbook page and filled with photos and ephemera.

10 Days To...
BY CAROL

Lay three lunch bags on top of each other, alternating the side which opens. Fold all bags in half. Open flat, then machine stitch the bags together on the fold line. Add papers and decorative elements to the pages. Fill pockets with travel ephemera, extra photos, etc.

VARIATIONS: The same type of book can be constructed using manila envelopes, small coin envelopes or any other type of structure with a side opening.

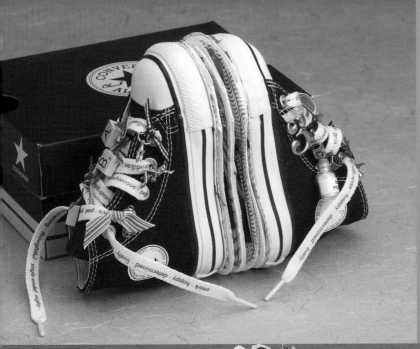

Footnotes
BY DEBBIE

THE PROCESS

Make a shoe-shaped accordion book by accordion folding paper, tracing a shoe, then cutting it out. If the paper is not long enough, add more sections and glue together, overlapping coordinating feet. Stamp backgrounds using other shoes with designs on the bottom. (Use a brayer to apply ink to the bottom of the shoes, then press paper to the shoe.) Stitch around each foot. Stamp each child's footprint on the back of the accordion. Add words to the shoelaces by using fabric transfers. Adorn with charms, ribbon and other assorted objects. Glue accordion ends to the bottom of the decorated shoes. Print a "logo" onto canvas paper, cut with a circle punch and glue over existing label.

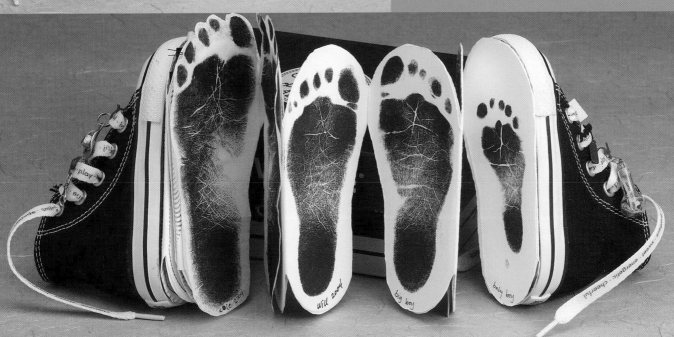

Consider yourself lucky! In the 7th century—B.C.—scribes had to engrave their recordings on clay tablets. And they couldn't sit and muse or the clay would harden. Fortunately, today, we have the luxury of writing—as leisurely as we please—in journals filled with paper. So take a minute to celebrate that privilege by creating a stunning book in which to divulge your innermost thoughts and feelings.

Childhood Memories Junque Book

BY CAROL

STEP 1: To create a "junque" book, use a craft knife to cut out the inside of an existing book. Be careful not to damage the spine when cutting through the binding.

STEP 2: Cover the front and back covers to the hinge area.

STEP 3: Cover the spine with a coordinating paper, overlapping the paper to the front and back cover papers. In this sample, the cover paper was created by weaving strips of cardstock to form a sheet large enough for the front cover.

STEP 4: Cover the inside of the book with end papers which extend into the spine area. Overlap the front and back end papers in the spine.

For the inside pages, create signatures from cardstock, text weight paper or watercolor paper. Sew signatures to the spine, using a pamphlet stitch (refer to chapter two for pamphlet stitch directions). Sew anywhere from one to three signatures, depending on the thickness of the spine.

Seasons Journal BY JANELLE

This journal started out as a 10" x 10" 7gypsies gatefold journal. Cut the front covers in half horizontally to create four sections. (The back cover is still intact.) Cut the interior pages to the same format as the cover by cutting them in half horizontally and vertically. Idea to note: For the winter cover, emboss the word "winter" into the metal, then paint with white acrylic paint. Sand away the paint with steel wool until the words appear.

VARIATIONS: Use this journal to record traditions, foods, activities and thoughts about each season. It could also be used as a journal for someone who has four kids, to record four different vacations taken in a year or to document four areas of one's life such as religion, family, personal interests, accomplishments, etc.

THE PROCESS

Proverbs for Life BY RENEE

Cut 8 1/2" x 11" papers in half. Punch holes along the edge and tie with ribbon. Create various pockets for scripture strips and inserts.

the process

Personal Diary and Box of Alyssa

BY TENA

Diary

Use two pieces of 5" x 7" chipboard for the front and back covers. Cover with paper and embellishments. Make filler pages using 5" x 7" pieces of cardstock, vellum and patterned and lined paper. Staple cardstock tabs to the edge of the page. Leave a 1/2" free edge to accommodate a coil binding. When the book is assembled, bind at a copy store.

Box

Sand a wooden box, then prime with two coats of acrylic gesso. Allow to dry completely between coats. Paint with two coats of acrylic paint and allow to dry. Stamp top of box with embossing ink and heat emboss with silver embossing powder. Line inside top of box with cardstock and create a pocket to fill with assorted keepsakes. Adhere patterned paper inside the bottom using glossy Perfect Paper Adhesive. When dry, apply a coat of Perfect Paper over the top.

VARIATIONS: This project could be altered to create a "field book" and trinket box for a young boy. The field book could be used to draw pictures, write notes or clip pages from comic books and toy catalogs. The box could be used to store all the trash and treasures boys put in their pockets.

6 Books to Share with Others

Honor a new mom with a book of advice thoughtfully designed and compiled just for her. Have each friend create a page—a mini scrapbook page of sorts—to include in the book. And don't feel bound by a traditional cover; break free and experiment like Carol did with the cloth diaper. This collection of loving advice will certainly be a treasure for mom and baby.

forget the alarm clock

when you can

BY CAROL

BY JANELLE

a dose of humor

Thoughts

MY ADVICE TO YOU

love with vb 1 a : to hold dear : CHERISH

savor every moment

BY TENA

BE PATIENT

SAVOR EACH MOMENT

SLEEP WHEN YOU CAN

Welcome to motherhood my friend, you have embarked upon a lifelong journey that will lead you through emotions and experiences that will enrich your life and complete you in marvelous ways. Hold tight to the tiny hands that cling to you, and know that this precious new life you have brought into this world is unique and perfect. no other achievement in life could surpass it.

Babies are more trouble than you thought and more wonderful. Charles Osgood

A Baby is born with a need to be loved and never outgrows it. Frank A. Clark

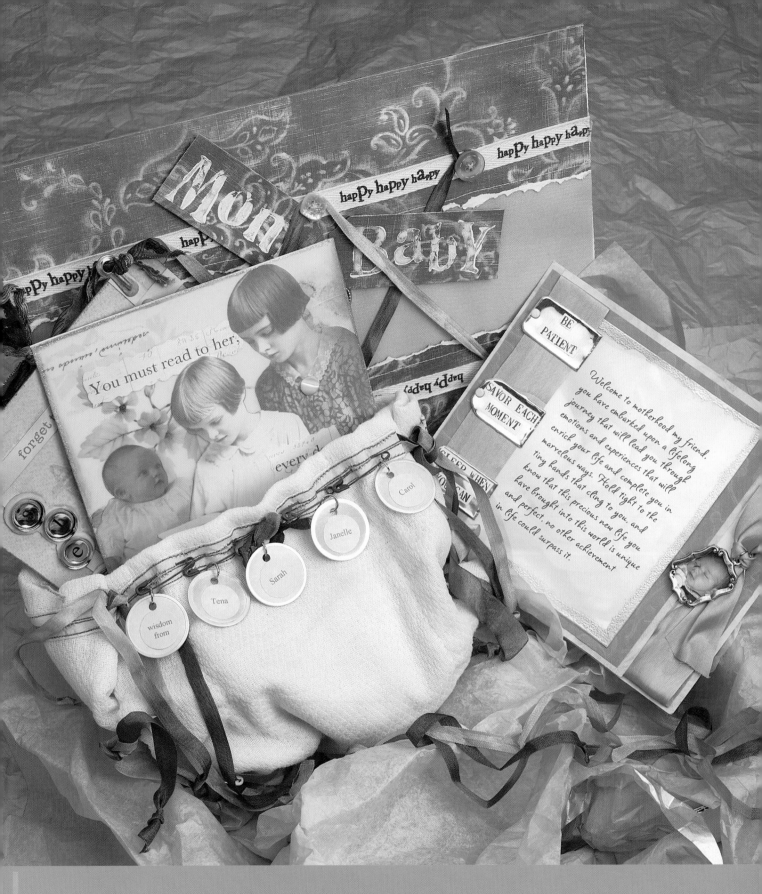

Advice For a New Mom
GIFT BOX, DIAPER AND CONCEPT BY CAROL

Form a diaper shape out of a cloth baby diaper. Secure the sides with ribbon. Add ribbon to leg sections; secure with mini safety pins.
Add title and contributors' names to tags, then affix to diaper with colored safety pins. Insert 6" x 6" advice panels into "cover."

VARIATIONS: Fill a 7gypsies house book with quotes, decorating advice, seed packs, etc. and slip it inside a paint can
for a cozy housewarming gift. Or fill fun containers with recipes and marriage advice for a new bride.

7 The Cover Story

Walk by any newsstand and you'll notice the striking covers competing for your attention. While it's supposed to be what's on the inside that counts, let's face it, a great cover is a real attention getter. The books in this chapter are no different. Our clever artists have turned these plain-jane, ready-made books into custom-crafted works of art. Don't judge a book by its cover? Yeah, right!

365 Days of Fabulous You

BY RUTH

Rubber stamp a title on the front of a mini planner and fill the inside with tributes to a child.

VARIATIONS: Use a mini planner to show a timeline for a pregnancy, engagement or other significant event.

the process

Garden Book

BY CAROL

Paint two coats of gesso over the existing cover. Allow to dry between coats. When dry, paint over gesso with antique-white paint. Stamp a diamond pattern over entire cover. Add decorative elements such as buttons and beads. Stamp the title on cardstock, punch out and glue to the underside of clear buttons. Add ribbon to the spine. Cover handle with tissue and cigar labels. Tie ribbon around handle to cover metal parts.

THE PROCESS

Discover Journal BY DEBBIE

Machine stitch fabric squares to the front of a plain journal. Embellish with assorted ephemera.
Glue paper to the back of clear buttons, then sew to the cover.

THE PROCESS

Precious Memories
BY RENEE

"Quilt" several colors of cardstock by adhering them to white copy paper, then sewing along the "seams." Adhere to the front of a Kolo album. Stamp and emboss to embellish. Stitch accents to ends of ribbon.

VARIATIONS: This album is great for a baby gift. Re-create a similar album for other occasions by simply changing the color scheme. Unique tie possibilities include bead chain, braided ribbons, elastics, twine or raffia.

Dreamer
BY SARAH

Sand the cover of a blank book. Glue strips of dictionary pages to the cover, then cover with a layer of Diamond Glaze diluted with water. While still wet, sprinkle ultra-fine glitter on top. When dry, add another coat of thinned-down Diamond Glaze. Adhere metal garden gate and clamp in place until dry. Brush Diamond Glaze on gate, then sprinkle glitter on top. Use Lazertran to transfer a collaged image to a tile, then adhere to gate.

VARIATIONS: Instead of the metal gate, paint, transfer or collage a piece of wood or metal, adding a small decorative plate on top. A framed photo would also look neat on top.

Play
BY CAROL

Use parts from an unwanted game board to create a theme cover for a journal. In this sample, pieces from a Monopoly box cover were cut and placed onto a pre-purchased spiral bound journal. The theme is "play" and the journal is filled with vacations to various locations depicted by Monopoly real estate cards.

Wine Journal
BY JANELLE

Cover part of a ready-made wine journal with paper. Make book belts from ribbon and silver locks. Pin words to a strip of cork adhered to the top. For the "wine journal" label, rubber stamp directly on a small ceramic tile, then glue on the decorative leaves. Cut a square of Wonder Tape to fit over the tile and add glass beads to the top and mini silver beads to the bottom.

"When we are collecting books, we are collecting happiness." If what author Vincent Starrett said is true, than we can, in a way, bestow the gift of happiness to loved ones when we add to their collection with a handcrafted book. Whether you quickly transform a ready-made book into a personal treasure or lovingly construct one of the simple books featured in this chapter, when filled with thoughts, photos and trinkets, it will be cataloged as a favorite gift!

Love Travels

BY TENA

Cover the inside and outside of a plain pocketed folio with paper. Bind the edges of the folio and the inside of the spine with black gaffers tape. Use tags to create "miss you" and "love you" coupons. Make a belt closure by stitching bias tape with a contrasting color thread. Loop the bias tape around metal rings and machine stitch to secure.

VARIATIONS: This folio would be great for someone going on a trip to remind them of the special people at home. It would also make a great gift for Grandma when the new baby arrives or try using it as a party favor for a special birthday or anniversary.

THE PROCESS

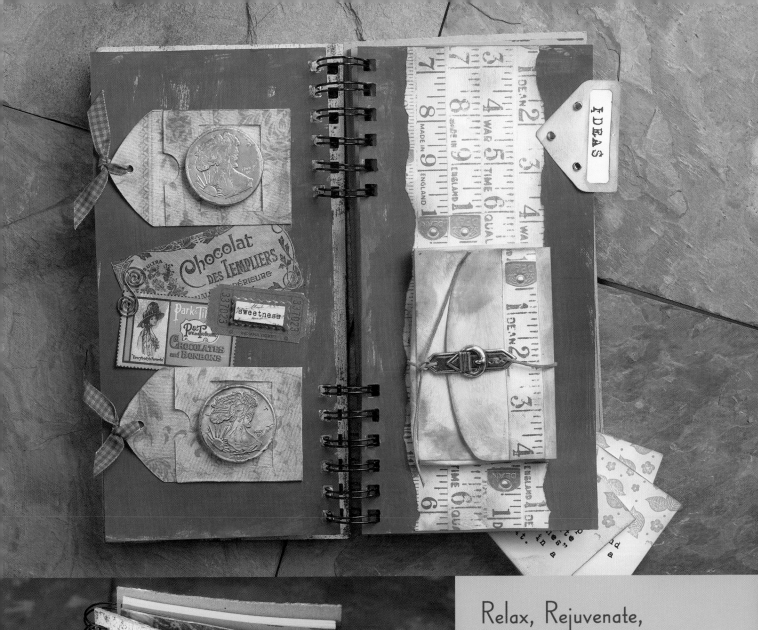

Relax, Rejuvenate, Restore

BY CAROL

Embellish the cover of a ready-made spiral journal. This sample was painted, then aged with crackle medium to resemble old wood. Add words, elements and ephemera in keeping with the theme of the book.

VARIATIONS: Create pouches, portfolios, slip-in pockets and envelopes to house thoughts, ideas, bath salts, tea bags, recipes, candy, etc. What a fun time the recipient will have discovering all of the hidden treasures!

the process

Best of Times Book Frame
BY DEBBIE

Cover the front of a book with tissue paper, then embellish. Glue metal corners to a piece of glass. Make small holes in the cover with an awl and attach the glass with small barbed elastics.

VARIATIONS: Choose a book to match the event of the gift. A baby book would make a great frame for a baby shower or a map book would be great for travel photos.

Kid Like You

BY SARAH

Paint the cover with Lumiere. When dry, rub the edges with gold metallic rub-ons. Cover the title block with a sepia-toned photo printed on a transparency. Secure the transparency with pearl straight pins. Attach a slightly larger pearl bead to the other end of each pin with Diamond Glaze.

For the "Sunny Vacation" page, paint a two-page spread with Lumiere. When dry, rub the edges with gold rub-ons. On the left-hand page, frame a square of red patterned paper with a square of wallpaper. Paint jute with Lumiere, then tie to the page with waxed linen. Adhere sea glass over the jute with Diamond Glaze. Collage photos and seashell images on the right-hand page.

VARIATIONS: The ideas shown on this spread could easily be adapted to any family recollection. If using cloth for a background, use a scrap from something actually worn or use buttons from your Great-grandma's button tin.

9 Before You Throw it Away

Altering books isn't a new rage. In fact, a form of altered books has been around since the 11th century when Italian monks scraped the ink off vellum manuscripts and added new text and illustrations on top. Done mostly for economic purposes, this technique—called palimpsest—has found its way into 21st century book arts. So start scraping, painting and altering to create fascinating masterpieces for your memories.

Lauren
BY CAROL

Sand the pages of a children's board book to remove the glossy surface, then paint the pages and edges with white gesso. Sponge chalk inks over the top. Add photos, letters and stamped images so the images show through the cut out areas. (The cut outs were part of the original book). Embellish with buttons, ribbon and charms.

Le Bebe

BY JANELLE

Cover a book with paper, smoothing with a brayer. Embellish as desired. Create a closure belt with ribbon attached with studs and glue. For the "Baby Photos" page, create a title block on the left page. Paint the opposite page white and insert a mini-folder book in the book. Set an eyelet on the side of each folder, tying ribbon through each one. Make the "Baby" page by tying hooks through several pages using twine. Adhere ribbon to the page to cover the tops of the hooks. Sew loops onto photos and hang from the hooks. Add journaling and title.

Defining Moments

THE PROCESS

BY CAROL

Dismantle a book according to the directions for the junque book in chapter five. Glue fabric to front, back and outside edge of spine. Allow the edges of the fabric to remain raw. Glue coordinating fabric to interior book ends and inside of spine. Cut and fold paper to make three signatures. Tie the signatures to the spine with ribbon. Stagger the position of the knots on the outside of the book. Add charms. To make the interior "honeycomb" book, stack several coin envelopes. Between each envelope, apply glue in an oval pattern from the top to the bottom of the envelope. Place a weight on the stack and allow to dry. When dry, adhere the top of the stack to the left side of a two-page spread and the bottom to the facing page. When the page is opened, the "book" will resemble a honeycomb. Interior pages shown on right. ➤

Collection of Cousins

BY TENA

These books started out as a set of Winnie The Pooh board books found on a bookstore sale table. Lightly sand board books and carrying case. Paint two coats of gesso onto all surfaces. Allow to dry completely between coats. Spray paint the handle of the case. Use acrylic paints to streak color onto exterior of books and case to create desired effects. Rubber stamp book titles and journaling on books and carrying case. Brush Mod Podge over all painted and stamped surfaces to seal the paint. Adhere photos on covers and carrying case.

VARIATIONS: Use this concept to create a set of books showing a child's favorite toys. This would also be a cute set to make for a Grandma, with one book for each group of Grandchildren. It would also be fun to have each book in the set be representative of a different vacation spot and then decorate the case like a suitcase.

credits

Products without a credit are either part of the artist's personal stash or not available for purchase.

NOTE: All walnut ink is from 7gypsies. And unless otherwise noted, all computer fonts are downloaded from the Internet. 2Peas fonts are downloaded from www.twopeasinabucket.com and CK fonts are from Creating Keepsakes.

Chapter 1
Books, Incorporated
PAGES 4-11

JAGGER

STEEL END, PENDANT BOX, SPIRALES, GOLD CLOCKS, RECTANGLE AND PRINTED TWILL: 7gypsies
EYELETS: Making Memories

OUR VANCOUVER MESS

LETTER STAMPS: Hero Arts
PATTERNED PAPER: Anna Griffin
RUBAN: 7gypsies

DISCOVERING AGE 2

PAPER, "2," WORD STICKERS, PHOTO TURNS, INDEX TAB AND CLASP: 7gypsies
TYPEWRITER-KEY LETTERS: Li'l Davis Designs
IVORY LETTERS: Westrim Crafts
RIBBON: Memory Lane
ENAMELED EMBLEM: www.collagejoy.com
EYELET: Making Memories
ENVELOPE DIE CUT: Ellison

FACES BY YOU

RUBBER STAMPS: Stampers Anonymous, Paper Inspirations and Wisecracks
RIBBON AND SNAPS: Making Memories

DESTINATION FLORIDA

PAPER: 7gypsies and Making Memories
TISSUE PAPER: 7gypsies
RUBBER STAMPS: www.junque.net, Club Scrap, Yosogo and Hampton Art Stamps
HAT PIN, METAL SNAPS, RUB-ONS AND BOOK PLATE: Making Memories
FIBERS: Timeless Touches
CHALK: Craf-T Products
PAINT: Twinkling H20's, Angelwings Enterprises
OVERSIZED SLIDE MOUNTS: FoofaLa
PHOTO CORNERS: Canson
BUTTON: Coats & Clark

EVERY BOY SHOULD HAVE A DOG

PAPER: Bazzill Basics, 7gypsies and Carolee's Creations
SNAPS, SAFETY PINS, HAT PINS AND STAPLES: Making Memories
MINI BRADS: Lost Art Treasures
BRASS SQUARE AND CIRCLE FRAMES: Ink It!
GOLD BRADS: Office Max
MINI BRAD: Lost Art Treasures
RUBBER STAMPS: PSX Design, Hero Arts, Yosogo, Ma Vinci's Reliquary and Hampton Art Stamps
CHALK: Craf-T Products
SEWING THREAD: Coats and Clark

THIRD GRADE

PAPER: Bazzill Basics, American Crafts, Design Originals and Karen Foster
WOODEN LETTER DISCS: Li'l Davis Designs
EXTREME EYELETS AND RUB-ON LETTERS: Creative Imaginations
BEAD CHAIN: Making Memories
RUBBER STAMPS: Hero Arts, Eclectic Omnibus and Ma Vinci's Reliquary
PAINT: Delta

LITTLE BUMP

SPIRALES, PRINTED TWILL, HARDWARE, TISSUE PAPER, MAGNETIC PLATE, NICKEL STUD, TYPEWRITER KEY, VINTAGE LABEL AND WAXED LINEN: 7gypsies
EYELETS: Making Memories

SPLENDOR AND GRANDEUR

PAPER: 7gypsies, Karen Foster and Li'l Davis Designs
TISSUE PAPER: DMD
BOOK PLATE AND ALUMINUM TAG: Anima Designs
ELASTIC: 7gypsies
GLASS RODS: Stampington & Company
FRAME: Maude & Millie
CHARMS: Fancifuls, Inc.
"WONDER" LABEL: me & my BIG ideas
COMPUTER FONT: 1942 Report
RUBBER STAMPS: Rubber Baby Buggy Bumpers and PSX Design
MESH: Magic Mesh
LEAVES: Nature's Pressed
WAXED COTTON: Memory Lane
MINI BRADS: Coffee Break Design
ACCORDION INSERTS: Papers by Catherine

BRAND NEW ME

PAPER: National Cardstock and Paper Adventures
CHIPBOARD: Memory Lane
SILK FLOWERS: Michael's
MINI BRADS: Lasting Impressions
PHOTO TURN: 7gypsies
PRONG FASTENERS: ACCO
RUB-ON LETTERS: Creative Imaginations
RUBBER STAMPS: Ma Vinci's Reliquary and Yosogo

HOLLYWOOD ROMANCE

LAYERS, NAILHEADS, BUCKLE AND LONG BAR: 7gypsies
PAPER: Bazzill Basics and 7gypsies
RUBBER STAMPS: PSX Design and Ma Vinci's Reliquary
METALLIC RUB-ON'S: Craf-T Products
BEADS: Beader's Paradise

HANA

PAINT: Plaid
PAPER: Bazzill Basics, 7gypsies and Cross My Heart
RUBBER STAMPS: PSX Design
TAG AND COIN ENVELOPES: Waste Not Paper
ART KEEPER: Renaissance Art
BARBED ELASTICS, CLOCK, BOX CLOSURE, SPIRALE, SILVER BUCKLE AND BARS: 7gypsies

BABY DELANIE

PAPER: Anna Griffin and Magenta
HINGES, RUB-ONS, RIBBON AND FLOWER
BRADS: Making Memories
RUBBER STAMPS: Impress Rubber Stamps,
Postmodern Design and Anna Griffin
WORD CHARMS: Li'l Davis Designs
PEWTER CHARM: Nunn Design
BUTTONS: Junkitz
STYLE STONES: Clearsnap
HEART FRAME: Scrapworks
PEWTER HEART: Stampington & Company
PRINTED TWILL: 7gypsies
PAINT: Plaid

Chapter 2
No Matter How You Fold It
PAGES 12-15

THE ADVENTURES OF ZANDER & MILES

PRINTED TWILL, WIRE CONNECTOR, KEY,
ALLIGATOR CLIP, TYPEWRITER KEYS,
CLOTHES PIN, WAXED LINEN, BELT LOOPS
AND PAPER: 7gypsies
JUMP RINGS: Making Memories
RIVET: Chatterbox
METAL FRAMES: Scrapworks
ALPHABET DISCS: Chronicle Books

EXPLORING LAS VEGAS

ACCORDION BOOK: K & Company
PAPER: Anna Griffin
RUB-ON LETTERS: Creative Imaginations
ELASTICS: 7gypsies
COMPUTER FONT: 2Peas Submarine

FOR MY MUM

VELLUM: Autumn Leaves
PAPER: 7gypsies and Wordsworth
METALLIC RUB-ONS: Craf-T Products

FREEDOM

VINTAGE TIN: Memory Lane
BEAD CHAIN AND EYELETS:
Coffee Break Design
COPPER LETTERS: K & Company
WAXED LINEN, LAYERS AND PAPER:
7gypsies
DEFINITIONS: Making Memories
ALPHABET STAMPS: JudiKins
ACRYLIC GESSO: Liquitex

WAITING FOR THE TRAIN

PAPER AND NAIL HEADS: 7gypsies
MINI BRADS: American Tag Co.
HINGES: Making Memories

SCHOOL DAYS

PAPER: 7gypsies, Magenta and
K & Company
FABRICS AND ESCUTCHEON: Ink It!
PEWTER NUMBER, OVAL FRAME AND
RUBBER BAND: 7gypsies
ACCORDION INSERTS: Papers by Catherine
LETTERS: K & Company
SEA GLASS: Alicia G.
LABEL HOLDER, DEFINITION AND EYELET
WORD: Making Memories
COPPER DISK: Nunn Design
PAGE POINTS: Levenger
ENVELOPE: EK Success

MY FAMILY CONNECTIONS

ACCORDION BOOK, PAPER, WAXED LINEN,
SAFETY PIN, BLACK TWILL, TAG, GARTERS,
BLANK LABELS, PHOTO TURNS AND
JEWELRY LABELS: 7gypsies
"DRIVE" LABEL: Cavallini Papers
RUBBER STAMPS AND STENCIL:
Ma Vinci's Reliquary
RIBBON: Making Memories
PEWTER BRACELET, PEWTER HANGER, BELT
BUCKLE AND CORNERS: Maude and Millie
TYPEWRITER LETTERS: EK Success
RIBBON, PEWTER WORD PLATE AND
HEART CHARM: Memory Lane
PAINT: Plaid
RED METAL TAG: Queen of Tarts
METAL STENCIL NUMBER:
Li'l Davis Designs
EYELETS AND BRADS: Coffee Break Design

Chapter 3
The Extremes
PAGES 16-19

FACES OF MY FAMILY

TAGS: American Tag
PAPER: KI Memories
RIBBON AND TIN: Memory Lane
PORCELAIN FACE: Ink It!

LITTLE MISS MILLIE

RIBBON AND DOMINOS: 7gypsies
JUMP RING: Making Memories

FRANCE TRAVEL JOURNAL

RIBBON AND VELLUM ENVELOPE:
Memory Lane
MAP AND PEWTER STICKERS:
Stampington & Company
TAG, LAYER, MAGNETIC PLATE, ENAMEL
PLATE, SILVER CLIP, SPIRALE, TWILL AND
WAXED LINEN: 7gypsies
BOOK LOCKET: Ink It!
PAINT: Plaid
EIFFEL TOWER DIE CUT: Li'l Davis Designs
RUBBER STAMPS: Stampers Anonymous,
Angie-B, Stamp Francisco, Stampa Rosa
and Denami Design
BOOK PLATE: *Decorative Ornaments &
Alphabets* by Henry Lewis Johnson
DRAWER PULL: Home Depot

WEDDING PHOTO BOOK

SPIRALES AND WIRE CONNECTOR:
7gypsies
PHOTO CORNERS AND FRAME: Details
FAUX WAX SEAL: Sonnets, Creative
Imaginations
RUBBER STAMPS: Hero Arts
FLOWERS: Jolee's Boutique

SPOOL BOOK

PAPER, WAXED LINEN, BARBED ELASTIC
AND RUBAN: 7gypsies
EYELET: Dritz
WOOD SPOOLS: Timber

TOOTH FAIRY

MATCHBOX: Silver Crow Creations
WATCHMAKER TIN: Memory Lane
PAINT: Delta
DRAWER PULLS AND DOOR KNOCKERS:
FoofaLa
SPIRALE: 7gypsies
RUBBER STAMPS: Yosogo, PSX Design
and Junque
PAPER: American Crafts
BRADS AND BEAD CHAIN:
Making Memories
SMALL ENVELOPE: Hero Arts

Chapter 4
Unexpected Elements
PAGES 20-23

BAND-AID FOR THE HURT

TINKER PIN: 7gypsies
WORD PUDDLES: K & Company
CHARMS: My Weakness
ACRYLIC GESSO: Liquitex

RADMAN'S TAG BOOK

TAG, PAPER, SPIRALES, WATCH FACE,
ELASTIC AND WAXED LINEN: 7gypsies
RUBBER STAMPS: Hero Arts

GRANDMA'S BRAG BOOK

TAGS, PAPER, ELASTIC, SPIRALE AND
WAXED LINEN: 7gypsies

FAMILY ROAD TRIP

PAPER: Memory Lane
MAP: AAA Arizona
RIVETS, WASHERS AND PIANO HINGE:
Home Depot
BOTTLE CAPS: ARTchix Studio
BRASS KEY, COMPASS AND HAND
CHARM: Ink It!
SCRABBLE TILES, ELASTIC AND CLOCK
FACE: 7gypsies
WIRE AND LETTER BEADS: Westrim Crafts
FLEXIBLE MICROSCOPE SLIDES: FoofaLa
BRADS: Lost Art Treasures
NAME PLATE: Magic Scraps
ALPHABET LETTERS: Colorbök
CLAY BEADS: Gary M. Burlin & Co.
CHARMS: QVC
PAINT: Delta
CHALK: Craf-T Products
METAL TAG: Making Memories
RUBBER STAMPS: PSX Design,
Yosogo and JudiKins
COMPUTER FONTS: Facelift and
2Peas Essential

GO FIGHT WIN

PAPER: Bazzill Basics
LETTER STICKERS AND BUBBLE WORDS
AND NUMBERS: Creative Imaginations
RUBBER STAMP: Ma Vinci's Reliquary
METAL LOCKER BOOK: Barnes and Noble
POETRY WORD BEADS:
www.magneticpoetrybeads.com
TRANSPARENCY: Apollo
ALPHABET LETTERS: Colorbök

10 DAYS TO...

PAPER: Li'l Davis Designs
TYPEWRITER-KEY FRAMES, WORDS,
SPIRALE, TISSUE PAPER, PEWTER FRAME
AND RUBAN: 7gypsies
CRAFTING ALUMINUM AND RUB 'N BUFF:
Amaco
BRADS AND EYELETS: Making Memories

FOOTNOTES

WATERCOLOR PAPER: Canal Montreal
CANVAS PAPER: Strathmore
RIBBON: 7gypsies, May Arts and Makuba
WAXED LINEN: 7gypsies
STAMPING INK: Ranger Industries
and Memories
LABEL MAKER: Dymo
SPIRALE, BEAD BOTTLE, INK BOTTLE,
LETTERS AND KEY: 7gypsies
METAL CHARMS: Ink It!
TRANSFER PAPER: June Tailor

Chapter 5
Books for Self Expression
PAGES 24-27

CHILDHOOD MEMORIES JUNQUE BOOK

PAPER: Anna Griffin, Carolee's Creations
and Design Originals
CORNERS AND DRAWER PULLS:
Maude and Millie
OPTICAL LENS AND BRASS TAG:
ARTchix Studio
TAGS, TWILL, WAXED LINEN, PHOTO
TURNS AND RUBAN: 7gypsies
LIBRARY POCKET AND CARD: Anima
Designs
CLOCK HAND: Limited Edition
RUBBER STAMPS: Hampton Art Stamps
and Postmodern Design
HINGES AND LABEL HOLDER: Making
Memories
BRADS: Memory Lane
WORD STICKERS: K & Company
PAINT AND CRACKLE MEDIUM: Plaid
TRANSPARENCY: 3M
COMPUTER FONT: 1942 Report

SEASONS JOURNAL

JOURNAL, PAPER, LABEL, BOTTLE,
TASSEL, HARDWARE, PRINTED TWILL,
CLOCK, TINKER PINS, TAGS, PHOTO
TURNS, TWIGS AND RUBAN: 7gypsies
SNOWFLAKES, FLOWERS AND LEAVES:
Jolee's Boutique
EYELETS: Making Memories
RUBBER STAMPS: Hero Arts

PROVERBS FOR LIFE

RUBBER STAMPS: Stampin' Up!
and PSX Design
RUB-ON ALPHABET: Creative
Imaginations
COMPUTER FONT: Palatino Linotype
EYELETS: Making Memories
HANDMADE PAPER: Jennifer Handmade
Paper Collection
RUBAN: 7gypsies

PERSONAL DIARY AND BOX OF ALYSSA

PAPER: Memory Lane, 7gypsies, Autumn
Leaves, Forget Me Not Designs, EK
Success, K & Company and me and my
BIG ideas
CHIPBOARD: Memory Lane
RIBBON: Offray
TACS AND SNAPS: Chatterbox
NAILHEADS: Jewelcraft
CLIPS, METAL FRAME, JUMP RINGS AND
METAL-RIMMED TAG: Making Memories
SLIDE MOUNTS: www.collagejoy.com
and FoofaLa
RUBBER STAMPS: PSX Design, Ma Vinci's
Reliquary, Hero Arts, Pepper Press and
Club Scrap
QUOTE STICKER: Wordsworth
MINI STAPLES: Swingline
GLASSINE ENVELOPE:
Ma Vinci's Reliquary
COIL BINDING: 7gypsies
ACRYLIC GESSO AND PAINT: Liquitex

Chapter 6
Books to Share With Others
PAGES 28-29

ADVICE FOR A NEW MOM

RUBAN AND SAFETY PINS: 7 gypsies
TAGS: American Tag
RIBBON: Memory Lane

Chapter 7
The Cover Story

365 DAYS OF FABULOUS YOU

MINI PLANNER: Franklin Covey
HEART CLASP, SILVER FRAME, NAILHEADS, BOX CLOSURE, WAXED LINEN AND PAPER: 7gypsies
RUBBER STAMPS: PSX Design and River City Rubber Works
METALLIC RUB-ONS: Craf-T Products

GARDEN BOOK

ACRYLIC GESSO: Liquitex
PAINT: Plaid
BUTTONS AND HANDLE: 7gypsies
RUBBER STAMPS: Impress Rubber Stamps and Postmodern Design
CIGAR LABELS: Queen of Tarts

DISCOVER JOURNAL

LAYERS, GYPSY PINS, PRINTED TWILL, LAUNDRIE BUTTONS, MINI TAGS, ELECTRIQUE, NAILHEAD, PRINTABLE FABRIC AND SPIRALE: 7gypsies

PRECIOUS MEMORIES

RUBBER STAMPS: Hero Arts, PSX Design, Stampers Anonymous and Rubber Moon

DREAMER

GLITTER: Pretty Prismas
METAL GATE: The Artist's Nook

PLAY

JOURNAL, PHOTO TURN, NAILHEADS, PRINTED TWILL AND WAXED LINEN: 7gypsies
PAPER: Cross My Heart, KI Memories and Anna Griffin
RUBBER STAMPS: PSX Design and Hero Arts
LETTER STICKERS: Wordsworth
LETTER BUTTONS: Junkitz

WINE JOURNAL

STEEL END, CLEAR WORDS, PAPER, RUBAN, ELASTIC, TINKER PINS, BAMBOO CLIPS, SILVER CLIP, NAILHEAD AND SILVER LOCK: 7gypsies
FAUX WAX SEAL: Sonnets, Creative Imaginations
RUBBER STAMPS: Hero Arts

Chapter 8
Books for Gifting

LOVE TRAVELS

PAPER: Memory Lane and K & Company
PLAIN FOLIO: River City Rubber Works
RIBBON: Offray, 7gypsies and Making Memories
METAL RING CLOSURE: 7gypsies
EXTREME EYELETS: Creative Imaginations
MINI BRAD: Lost Art Treasures
LETTER STICKERS AND LETTER TILES: me and my BIG ideas, Creative Imaginations and K & Company
TAGS AND POSTAGE LETTERS: FoofaLa
RUBBER STAMPS: PSX Design, Hero Arts and Yosogo
CHALK: Craf-T Products
BUTTON: Heartland Buttons

RELAX, REJUVENATE, RESTORE

JOURNAL, SPIRALE, STICKERS, WAXED LINEN, TYPEWRITER-KEY FRAMES AND INDEX TAB: 7gypsies
PAINT AND CRACKLE MEDIUM: Plaid
LABEL HOLDER AND SAFETY PIN: Making Memories
TYPEWRITER LETTERS: K & Company
COPPER CIRCLE LETTER: EK Success
RUBBER STAMP: Hero Arts and Rubber Baby Buggy Bumpers
OVAL CHARM: Nunn Design
DIE CUT TAG ENVELOPE AND MINI PORTFOLIO: Ellison
BUCKLE: Maude and Millie
RIBBON AND WAXED COTTON: Memory Lane
PAPER: 7gypsies and Anna Griffin
WORD STICKERS: K & Company
LABEL: FoofaLa
MINI BRADS: Coffee Break Design
COMPUTER FONT: 1942 Report
PAINT: Lumiere
METALLIC RUB-ONS: Craf-T Products

BEST OF TIMES BOOK FRAME

PAPER, TISSUE PAPER, BOOK CORNERS, PRINTED TWILL, NAILHEAD, RIBBON AND BARBED ELASTIC: 7gypsies

KID LIKE YOU

PAINT: Lumiere
METALLIC RUB-ONS: Craf-T Products
PAPER, LABEL, STICKERS AND WAXED LINEN: 7gypesies

Chapter 9
Before You Throw it Away

LAUREN

ACRYLIC GESSO: Liquitex
RUBBER STAMPS: Ma Vinci's Reliquary, Turtle Press, Stampington & Company, Missing Link Stamp Company, Inkadinkado and JudiKins
BUTTONS: Hillcreek Designs
VELLUM ENVELOPES: Anima Designs
PAPER: 7gypsies and KI Memories
CLEAR FRAME: K & Company
CHARM: Nunn Design

LE BEBE

RIBBON, NAILHEADS, ENAMEL PLATE, MINI SILVER FRAME, LAYER, PAPER, DOMINOS, LABELS AND TYPEWRITER WORDS: 7gypsies
METAL FRAME, EYELETS AND MINI BOOK: Making Memories
RUBBER STAMPS: Hero Arts
PAINT: Jacquard Products
HOOKS: Dritz

DEFINING MOMENTS

PHOTO TURNS, METAL RING, WATCH FACE, WATCH CHARM STUD AND KEY CHARM: 7gypsies
CLOCK HAND: Limited Edition
EYELETS: Making Memories
BUTTON: Hillcreek Designs
RUBBER STAMPS: JudiKins, Stampers Anonymous, Stampington and Company, A Stamp in the Hand, Acey Deucy, Limited Edition and Ma Vinci's Reliquary
QUILTING FABRIC, GLASS PUDDLE AND WIRE CHARMS: Ink It!

COLLECTION OF COUSINS

ACRYLIC GESSO: Liquitex
PAINT: Delta and Americana
SPRAY PAINT: Krylon
PHOTO CORNERS: Canson
RUBBER STAMPS: Ma Vinci's Reliquary

artists

CAROL WINGERT teaches paper and book arts workshops at Memory Lane. She has been regularly published in *Legacy* and *Creating Keepsakes* and won *Creating Keepsakes* Hall of Fame Honorable Mention in 2002 and 2003. She was a contributing artist to *Designing with Photos, Designing with Words* and *7gypsies in Paris* and has contributed to several books for Design Originals. She lives in Gilbert, Arizona, with her husband (and best friend), Vern, and their daughter, Ashley.

carol

An avid reader, Carol believes *Little Women* was highly influential in her life. She reveals that she wanted to be like Jo—strong, determined and someone who got things done.

SARAH FISHBURN is a collage artist whose art can be seen in many books including *7gypsies in Paris; Artists' Journals and Sketchbooks: Exploring and Creating Personal Pages; Altered Books, Collaborative Journals and Other Adventures in Bookmaking; True Colors: A Palette of Collaborative Art Journals; Creative Paper Techniques for Scrapbooks; Creative Photo Cropping for Scrapbooks* and more. It has also been published in *Memory Makers, Legacy* and *ARTitude*, and she has been the featured artist in numerous indie zines. Her work has shown in galleries throughout the Southwest. She teaches classes locally and nationally.

RUTH GIAUQUE lives in Gilbert, Arizona, with her brilliant husband, Eric, and their four adorable children: Hana, Mikenna, Christian and Noah. Ruth was a contributing artist in *7gypsies in Paris* and has been published in *Creating Keepsakes, Simple Scrapbooks* and *Paper Crafts Magazine* among others. Ruth's interests include playing with her kids, photography, paper arts, teaching workshops at Memory Lane, teaching the violin and working with all of the fascinating people she has encountered along the way.

sarah

Sarah loves *Winter's Tale* by Mark Helprin because it's the most amazing book about justice ever written and because of the Woola Woola boys.

ruth

Ruth's favorite book is *Jonathan Livingston Seagull* by Richard Bach because, at times, we all need flying lessons.

After becoming an inductee into the *Creating Keepsakes* Hall of Fame in 2002, RENEE CAMACHO became a frequently published artist in many scrapbook magazines including *Creating Keepsakes*, *Simple Scrapbooks*, *Crafts Magazine*, and *Scrapbooks Etc.* She was also a contributing artist to *Designing with Words* and has developed product for Autumn Leaves. To add to her busy schedule, Renee has three children and is active in her church.

TENA SPRENGER loves teaching scrapbooking and paper arts classes at Memory Lane. She has been published in *Legacy*, *Scrapbooks Etc.* and *Creating Keepsakes* and was inducted into the 2004 *Creating Keepsakes* Hall of Fame. Tena lives in Mesa, Arizona, with her wonderful husband, Mike, and their two children, Alyssa and Michael. Tena's interests include photography, paper arts, reading and tap dancing.

renee

Renee enjoys any book by James Patterson because of his catching verbiage and thrilling mysteries.

tena

Tena's favorite book is *Memoirs of a Geisha* by Arthur Golden because he transports and immerses her into the world in the story.

JANELLE SMITH currently lives in Salt Lake City with her husband, Zach, and their son, Zander. They are looking forward to welcoming another boy into their family this spring. Her loves include photography, spending time with family and fulfilling her ever-present urge to create! Her work has been featured in *Designing with Photos*, *Designing with Words* and *7gypsies in Paris*.

DEBBIE CROUSE is a veteran contributor to all the Autumn Leaves books: *Designing with Vellum*, *Designing with Notions*, *Designing with Texture*, *Designing with Photos*, *Designing with Words* and *7gypsies in Paris*. When she is not working on books, she is designing for 7gypsies. She lives in Mesa, Arizona, with her wonderful husband, Skip. They have four children and three gorgeous grandchildren.

janelle

Her favorite novel is whatever she happens to be reading at the moment. She becomes totally engrossed in whatever she is reading—to the point where the house is in shambles. After finishing the book, she donates or shelves the book and doesn't think about it again.

debbie

Right now her favorite book is *War and Peace*; it is just heavy enough, when placed on glued projects, to hold things down.

The Sophisticated Scrapbook Presents

DESIGNING WITH
NOTIONS

DESIGNING WITH
vellum

SCRAPBOOKS,
AND MORE.

The Sophisticated Scrapbook Presents

DESIGNING WITH
TEXTURE

Quote
UNQUOTE

designing
WITH
PHOTOS

inspire
imagine
discover

DESIGNING
with
Words

Jennifer Ditz McGuire

Renee Camacho

Debbie Crouse

Carol Wingert

Kristina Nicolai-White

Tracy Robinson

Lisa Russo

HAVE
HOLD
live
ADORE
CITRUS FAMILY
&
joy
SOUL
MATE

Inspiration and
ideas for adding
meaning to your
scrapbooks,
cards and gifts
through the
power of words.

7gypsies
Paris